La Mer
(The Sea)
Three Symphonic Sketches

Claude Debussy

DOVER PUBLICATIONS, INC.
Mineola, New York

Published in Canada by General Publishing Company, Ltd., 30 Lesmill Road, Don Mills, Toronto, Ontario.
Published in the United Kingdom by Constable and Company, Ltd., 3 The Lanchesters, 162–164 Fulham Palace Road, London W6 9ER.

Bibliographical Note

This Dover edition, first published in 1997, is a republication of music from an early French edition. The instrumentation list and glossary are newly added.

International Standard Book Number: 0-486-29848-5

Manufactured in the United States of America
Dover Publications, Inc., 31 East 2nd Street, Mineola, N.Y. 11501

CONTENTS

La Mer
Trois Esquisses Symphoniques
The Sea: Three Symphonic Sketches

(1903–5)

INSTRUMENTATION

2 Flutes [Grandes Flûtes, G^{des} Fl.]
Piccolo [Petite Flûte, P^{te} Fl.]
2 Oboes [Hautbois, H$^{tb.}$]
English Horn [Cor Anglais, Cor A.]
2 Clarinets in A, B♭("Si♭") [Clarinettes, Cl.]
3 Bassoons [Bassons, B^{ons}]
Contrabassoon [Contre-Basson, C.B^{on}]

4 Horns in F [Cors (*chromatiques*)]
3 Trumpets in F [Tromp(ettes)(*chromatiques*)]
2 Cornets in C [Cornets (à Pistons) (Ut)]
3 Trombones [Tromb.]
Tuba

Timpani [Timbales, Timb.]

Percussion
   Bass Drum [Grosse-Caisse, Gr. C.]
   Cymbals [Cymbales, Cymb.]
   Triangle [Trg.]
   Tam-Tam [T.-T.]
   Glockenspiel (or Celesta) [Glock.]

2 Harps [Harpe]

Violins 1, 2 [Violons, V^{ons}]
Violas [Altos]
Cellos [Violoncelles, V^{elles}]
Basses [Contrabasses, C. Basses C.B.]

Glossary of French Terms

accordez (sur): tune (to)
alto: viola
animé, animez: vivaciously
archet: bow
assez: quite
au mouvement: a tempo; back in (previous) tempo
autres: others
avec: with
à vide: open string
baguette de timb(ale): kettledrum stick
b(ass)on: bassoon
beaucoup: much
bouché, bouchez: with stopping
bouche fermée: sung with mouth closed
calme: calm
cédez: slacken
changez en: change to
chaque: each, every
chevalet: bridge (of string instrument)
cl(arinette): clarinet
contrebasse: double bass
cor angl(ais): English horn
cor (à pistons): (valve) horn, French horn
cuivré, cuivrez: with a forced, hard tone
cymb(ales): cymbals
cymb(ales) ant(iques): "ancient" cymbals, a special form of the instrument
dans: in
de plus en plus sonore et en serrant le mouvement: with more and more volume, while quickening the tempo
divisés (en; par): divisi; divided (into; by)
do: the note C
doux: softly
dureté: harshness
du talon: with the nut of the bow
en animant (surtout dans l'expression): becoming livelier (especially in expressiveness)

en augmentant: crescendo
encore plus: even more
en croisant: crossing the hands
en dehors: prominently
enlever: remove
en retenant: holding back
en s'éloignant davantage: growing more distant
en serrant: stringendo, speeding up
entrée: entrance
et: and
expressif: expressive
fin: end
fl(ûte): flute
gracieux: graceful
g(ran)de fl(ûte): flute
gr(osse)-c(aisse): bass drum
harpe: harp
hautb(ois): oboe
initial: initial, of the beginning
jusqu'à: up to
la: the note A
langueur: languor
léger, légèrement: lightly
lent: slow
lenteur: slowness
lointain: far away, distant
mailloche: mallet, stick
mais: but
marqué: marcato
même: same
mesure: measure
mettez: put (on)
mi: the note E
modéré: moderate
mouv(emen)t (du début): tempo (of the opening)
mouvementé: agitato
naturel: natural, normal
ôtez: remove

ou: or
part(ie): part
pendant: during
p(eti)te fl(ûte): piccolo
peu à peu (animé pour arriver à): gradually (livelier in order to reach)
plus (de): more
pointe: tip
pos(ition) nat(urelle) [OR: *ordinaire*]: normal position
préparez le ton de: prepare the key of
près de: near
presque: almost
pupitre: desk
ré: the note D
reprenez: resume, go back to
retardez: slow down
revenir progressivement au I°. tempo: return gradually to the first tempo
rythme: rhythm
rythmé: rhythmically
sans: without
sec: drily
serrez: speed up, stringendo

seulement: only
si: the note B
sol: the note G
sonore: resoundingly, with volume
souple: supple
sourdine: mute
soutenu: sostenuto
sur: on
tamb(our) m(ilitaire): snare drum
tam-tam: gong
timb(ale): kettledrum
touche: fingerboard
toujours: always
tous: all
très: very
tromp(ette à pistons): (valve) trumpet
tumultueux: tumultuous(ly)
uni(e)s: all together; no longer divisi
un peu (plus): a little (more)
vibrant: vibrating
v(iol)on: violin
v(iolonc)elle: cello
vite: quickly

I. De l'aube à midi sur la mer
From dawn to noon on the sea

1

12

II. Jeux de vagues
Play of waves

21
57
Gdes Fl.
p très léger
Cl.
p très léger
Bons
Cors
dim. molto
Cymb.
Glock.
1re et 2de Harpes
pp
arco
mp dim. molto
Div.
dim. molto

123

En animant beaucoup

En animant beaucoup

35 En animant beaucoup

III. Dialogue du vent et de la mer

Dialogue of the wind and the sea

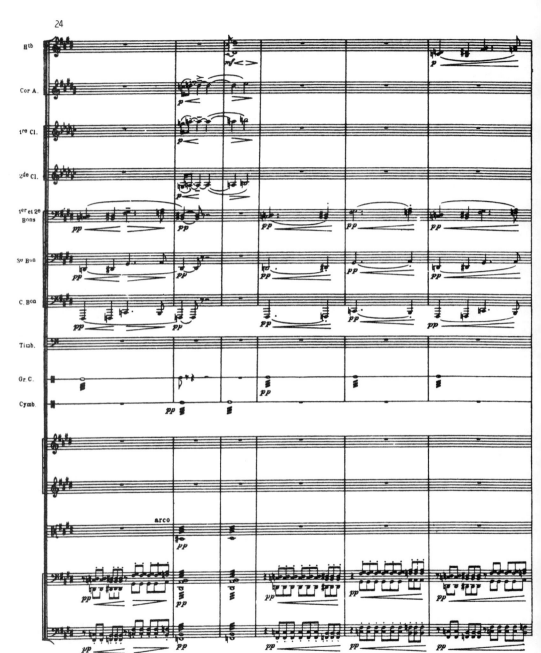

102

END OF EDITION